T0077895

KING OF TEAMS

How to Create Winning Teams
in an Unconventional Way

DAMON ALLISON SR.

Archway Publishing books may be ordered through booksellers or by contacting:

Archway Publishing
1663 Liberty Drive
Bloomington, IN 47403
www.archwaypublishing.com
844-669-3957

ISBN: 978-1-6657-1014-5 (sc)
ISBN: 978-1-6657-1015-2 (e)

Library of Congress Control Number: 2021915041

Print information available on the last page.

Archway Publishing rev. date: 07/30/2021

2013 National Champs

Super 64 Adidas Vegas Champs

Head Coach Damon Allison, Assistant Coach: Van Mayfield, Josh Kozinski, Jamal Popler, Jon Jon Williams, Fredrick Edmonds "Boo Man," Derrick Walton Jr, Jalen Hayes, Monte "Man Man" Morris, Quintan Harris, President and CEO Norm Oden, Assistant Coach Jeff Kozinski, Assistant Coach Brandon Berrett

Number One National Ranked Team

Head Coach Damon Allison, Assistant Coach: Van Mayfield, Assistant Coach Jeff Kozinski Demetrius Lake, Jermaine Jackson Jr, Adam Kozinski, Foster Loyer, Xavier Tillman, Isaiah Livers, James Beck Jr, Dylan Alderson, Jack Ballintine, Matthew Beachler

Powerhouse teams that I was a part of in the Corporate World:

Southwest Michigan First: Director of Economic Development

Zeigler Auto Group: Development of Aspiring Leadership and Recruiting

TESTIMONY & QUOTES ABOUT OUR JOURNEY

From Players and Coaches

Derrick Walton, Jr.: University of Michigan, LA Clippers, Detroit Pistons, and Philadelphia 76ers

"Falling in love with the grind and discipline is the key to success. It'll push you through days mentally and physically that you don't have the strength to do it!"

Isaiah Livers: University of Michigan, 2021 NBA Draft

"What made our team the best, was that we had expectations of being the best team. We were just a group of guys who loved the game of basketball. I remember our team being the most connected team every tournament. Win or lose we stayed by each other's side!"

Xavier Tillman: Michigan State University, Memphis Grizzles

"I feel like this squad was ultra-competitive. Nobody expected guys out of Michigan to turn into the best team in the country, but we did! Every one of us wanted to be the best. That's what pushed us to be so good together."

Matthew Beachler: Starting Shooting Guard at Central Michigan University

"It was a great experience to have a group of individuals come together as a team and fight for a common goal. We understood that if our team were successful, that individual accolades would come."

Coach Brandon Berrett: Head High School Basketball Coach, University Prep

"We were a great program because we followed each other's success. We made sure to stay close as coaches. All of our players were tight, and we were a family."

Mike Van Ryn
Director of Talent Development
Zeigler Auto Group

"Anyone who meets Damon instantly feels his passion for people. He has an innate ability to build relationships and is at his best when coaching and developing others. He truly cares about others and loves seeing them grow. He has been an instrumental part of our recruiting and development team at Zeigler Auto Group. I am so happy Damon achieved his goal of sharing his journey in his book."

Josh Kozinski: Central Michigan University Basketball #12

"Coach taught our team of kids how to become young men. Kids from all over the state and all different backgrounds. The coach was able to teach us the soft skills needed to be a TEAM rather than just individuals trying to make it to the next level. We all learned about respect, trust, communication, and becoming coachable. We all learned that for an individual to succeed, the team needed to succeed. I came onto that team as an individual looking to play ball. I left that team with a group of brothers I'll have forever."

Adam Kozinski: Central Michigan University Basketball #13

"Coach Allison was one of the best and hardest coaches I've ever had. He pushed me to be the best player I could be, on and off the court. He accepted me into a team that was bound to bring national attention, and I can't thank him enough for that. He showed me what it was like to be at the top level of the game of basketball. It shaped me into a great leader and a very hard worker. I learned many life lessons throughout the summers of basketball that we were together. Without Coach Allison, I would not be the man I am today. I am blessed to be part of that team but even more blessed to have a coach and mentor like him."

Jeff Kozinski: Michigan Mustangs Assistant Coach and Teacher at Edwardsburg High School (Josh and Adam's Dad)

"Coach Allison knows how to form great teams made up of individuals from all walks of life. When you can bring in talented individuals and get them to believe they are a part of something very special, it is done by installing a championship culture that is built with chemistry and Heart."

Jalen Hayes: Oakland University, Pro basketball Player, England

"Coach, I did not know you were writing a book about us and our time. That was an amazing time, Coach, an amazing time. It was great for us to be successful, win, and travel the country. That time, when I was 16 and 17 years old, taught me a lot about myself and how to build a brotherhood with my teammates and coaches."

Thomas Dillard III: High School State Champion with Kalamazoo Central, Played at University of Detroit, Assistant Coach Mustangs

"When Damon told me he was getting back into the Michigan Mustangs business and asked me to help, I had no idea that I wouldn't only be gaining a coaching partner, but another father to encourage and help develop my son, a therapist to help me work through the trials of life, and a brother as well. Tremendous dedication and sacrifice for all the young men that came through the program was an everyday occurrence, and I'm blessed to have been a part of it, 'The Mustang Way'"!

THE LEADERSHIP CONTRACT

I commit to bettering my best. I commit to finding a mentee and mentor to challenge my leadership. I commit to improving myself so that I can impact others to be great. I commit to people who need positive leadership, and I commit to the leaders who have shown me how to do right by them!

Sign Here:
First, Middle, and Last Name

We were all committed to each other to help kids.

INTRODUCTION

With a championship culture, you can feel the difference in the locker room. Suppose you have ever visited the Los Angeles Lakers organization or the Boston Celtics organization. In that case, I am sure you will feel the championship culture when you walk in. You will also have a feeling if you walk into the Washington Wizards or Cleveland Cavs organizations. However, it will feel completely different, and you will see/feel the difference between the two styles of Culture.

While competing, everyone wants to win. There's a process in learning how to win, though. While coaching at the highest level of youth basketball, I figured out the secret sauce to having the best chances to create winning teams. It starts with the correct Mindset. Having the right mindset will allow you to be adaptable to growing and changing when and where needed.

Along with the correct Mindset, three additional elements are the backbone of creating a championship team. They are the right Chemistry, Culture, and Heart. The combination of the three will give you the best opportunity for success in building a winning team.

A team with Chemistry will have a direct understanding of the Mindset of empathy for people. This type of team is dangerous because they will fight for the person in the seat next to them just as hard as they would fight for themselves. A team that understands how Chemistry works will also understand where a person will be resilient and have cohesiveness. With these elements, even if these teams lose, they will understand why and fix the mistakes that contributed to the loss, and turn those reasons into success stories.

A team that has a Culture-focused mindset will also be impactful. Culture gives a team the ability to see that everyone is in the same fight for a common purpose.

Having the Heart mindset is the final piece of the trifecta. No team will ever be a champion without Heart. Of course, people have their reasons as to why they want to compete. Maybe you are an underdog; perhaps you are fighting to be a breadwinner or just working for a paycheck. But, without Heart, the desire to execute any and every task, a competitor will fail 100% of the time.

Many coaches and leaders ask me questions like how I win and how I get players to play for me the right way?"

I tell them that I lead differently. With the Mindset of Chemistry, Culture, and Heart, my teams can conquer all challenges, or at least learn from them. I figured it out. I am the King of the Midwest in AAU basketball. Our team beat the best, and our program was on the top for an entire decade. We did it. We created the Vision and values of a winning team: Chemistry, Culture, and Heart.

As leaders, we have to have our Mindset on Chemistry, Culture, and Heart, but we must also align with our Vision and Values before guiding a team. Not knowing how we want to lead could directly impact our success or lack of it. My Heart allows me to teach in a way that lifts others and will enable them to lead with their talents and strengths.

How do we create the winning Vision? First, our team has to believe in themselves to be their best. That only happens if we can teach them to know their mission through a winning vision and core values. Therefore, it is imperative to ensure that the mission includes Vision and Values before the team member is selected.

When selecting teams, we need to identify each player's skills as a required asset to create Chemistry. After identifying these skills, we will start building the team. First, we need to make sure that the person has the proper "heartbeat." When looking to see if the player has Heart, we look for personality and responsibility. These tell us who the winners are and have the Mindset driven by Heart before they sign on.

Over the past 25 years, I have found myself feeling great, and I have also found myself struggling with thoughts of how I will "win in life." In many cases, teams win championships because they have winning in their DNA. A blueprint passed on to the next in line. I am not from a winning family, Culture, or mentality. My blueprint did not come with the XY chromosomes of winning DNA. Instead, I am of the "I want that culture, so I'm going to get it by any means necessary" Mindset.

This book uses lessons learned from my childhood, teenage hurdles, and championship-winning experiences to shorten the learning time for someone else. It's for future leaders, so they don't have to make the same leadership mistakes I did. I always promised that I would share my leadership if I figured out how to win consistently. I would give it to anyone who wanted to grow. My goal in life was to find my purpose, and now that I have, I want to share It. You are reading this book because you are a leader and want to take your leadership to another level by looking at Culture, Chemistry, and Heart as your templates for Team Building. The formula I outline here will help you use your experiences, cut through the smoke, and start using your leadership style.

People say that there is no book to being a great parent, coach, leader, or mentor. Well, close out all of the white noise and lock-in. This book will give parents, coaches, community leaders, and mentors light at the end of the tunnel. If you want to be a champion, finishing this book will allow you to be the expert in creating winning teams.

1

THE REASON BEHIND MY WHY

Creating winning teams is a passion of mine. I'm not only passionate about the process; I love it and live it in every facet of my life. If you can do the things you like and make yourself happy, you will reach your maximum potential. We are creatures of habit. So, we have to be thoughtful about doing things that create an outstanding balance. Using the right balance, we will win every time.

I've been waiting for the right time to bring my inner thoughts and top qualities to the world of writing. What better time to get started than now? I started writing this book during the COVID-19 Pandemic. I was living in Illinois and decided it was time to focus my Mindset on a clear vision and core values. While reflecting on my life, I realized how important balance is.

The Pandemic revealed apparent national issues, especially around social and racial injustice. During that time, I started reaching out to the people who mean the most to me—my extended family members, coaches, former colleagues, and all of my former basketball players—making sure everyone was doing the best they could. Many conversations revealed people talking about starting a business or getting ready to create some form of team. My thoughts were to build a template to give them a leadership guide to building teams before starting their venture.

I wrote this book for two different reasons. First, I am dyslexic and wanted to overcome the challenges of reading and writing upside down and backward. Overcoming hurdles and challenges are significant to me. It gives me fuel. Second, I wrote this book so people can understand how to choose the right teams and maximize their team's potential.

I was born and raised on the east side of Detroit. That's where I gained my "heart" and will to fight for myself. I am a father of four, a husband of 20 years, and a coach of Amateur Athletic Union (AAU) National Basketball Champion Teams. One of my lifelong dreams was to win a National Championship. Another was to graduate college so that I could be a classroom teacher and coach basketball. I accomplished those goals.

I graduated from Western Michigan University with a bachelor's degree in education, then returned to WMU to earn my master's degree in educational leadership. Once I accomplished those obstacles, I started soul searching again.

When I found out in 2014 that I had Dyslexia, a fire sparked within me. I didn't know why I was always the last to finish reading in class when I was younger. I never retained what I read, and, my goodness, spelling tests just killed me. Having Dyslexia has been challenging throughout my lifetime, especially reading upside down and backward. It's not a great feeling.

I love going against the odds, so overcoming this challenge by writing a book became my goal. Inspiring people, earning both a bachelor's degree and a master's degree while dealing with this learning disability—along with finishing this book--are huge personal milestones.

My family is my "WHY." My wife, Katherine Chelsea Allison, is my rock, my superhero. She changed the world as I knew it when I met her. She works in Human Resources at UPS, so she was considered an essential worker during the Pandemic. I met Chelsea in 2001 while visiting my best friend, who lived steps away from her. She and I connected right away and married a year and a half later. We will celebrate our 20th anniversary in June of 2022.

My oldest child, Tajanae, is my twin, in looks and spirit. We share the same drive and leadership traits. We see what we want and strive to get it. Sometimes people will say, "Your dreams are not attainable." Taj and I get excited about those types of challenges.

She's a beautiful young lady who is very talented in both running track and drawing. She qualified and competed in Track and Field at the Junior Olympics for seven years in a row, and her running skills have afforded her a scholarship at Indiana Tech. Of my four children, she has the most natural athletic ability.

Damon Jr, my oldest son, goes by DJ. He is my warrior, the fighter of the family. He watched me coach basketball and win national championships and wanted to be on one of those teams. Unfortunately, he did not have the skill set to get him there at the time. But he was so determined to be a great basketball player, and he stretches himself and works extremely hard. He is my comeback kid.

Finally, there are my eleven-year-old twins, Kalen and Jayden. The boys are the sweetest, kindest souls you will ever come across. They also love to learn and share a love for math and science. Their superpower is making people feel loved and special. It is a lot of fun to watch them grow and embrace learning new things. Because they are twins, they were born as a team, and they have a fantastic way of naturally understanding how to get the best out of others.

Because of my past coaching experiences, many people ask if I plan to put the twins in basketball. My response is always that I would be more than happy to, but they will make their own decisions on what activities they choose. At this point, they like to run track, football, soccer, and rock climbing. So it is beautiful watching them explore different interests for as long as they can and would like.

A Note to My Family:

I love you very much and am writing this book because I love the hurdles we've overcome together. I hope to continue to show you that you can do anything you put your mind to. I value and love everything you're fighting for and will always support your dreams and help you fight to get them. DJ, you're a great basketball player and have earned all of your success. Taj, I see all the Heart and hustle you have inside you and know you'll be great in life. Kalen and Jayden, I'm just overwhelmed with love and joy from all of you every day. I know you'll have an impact and leave a legacy in this world. Chelsea, you showed me what hard work and the pursuit of happiness are. You gave me life when we first met. I love you so much! Thank you for always supporting me and loving me through everything.

2

HEART: FIGHTING THE GOOD FIGHT

Sometimes we are dealt a bad hand, but in life, we still have to play. We can't just quit. Each person has 24 hours in a day, and it's up to us what we do with these hours. Growing up, I had exposure to so many things that could have been a death sentence. But, instead, I chose to be different. I decided to lean in on the good in my life. This decision is intentional. I chose a victory over victim mentality.

Losing my uncle Garmel to gun violence was the most challenging part of my childhood, partly because he had introduced me to basketball. Witnessing gun violence in the Black community as a child meant I had to develop a Heart bone at that point in my life to function.

Garmel Williams
October 29, 1975 - March 14, 1992

My neighbors, Mr. and Mrs. Oglasbe, helped me develop a sense of God and goodwill. They introduced me to Church. Every weekend, I would either stay at their house on Saturday night, so I didn't have to worry about getting there Sunday morning, or I would show up at their back door at 7:30 A.M. on Sunday. Mr. and Mrs. O were very cool. They loved all the kids in the neighborhood and pushed to save us all. I believed in God and thought that Church would help me, so I attached to the Oglasbes and Church. My family believed in Church and spoke about going, but Mr. and Mrs. O were living it. As a result, I felt stronger when I put God first.

Creating the Mindset and understanding your "why" is important in the initial stages of forming a team.

Some people in my life did drugs but did their best to keep me away from them. I had gang members in my life who also cared and chose to keep that life away from me. I also had Mrs. O and the Church, insisting that I trusted in God when trouble was staring me in the face.

The reality is that we can be successful no matter where we come from or our surroundings. But we have to use our 24 hours to the best of our ability. We have to lean on mentors, neighbors, and the people around us. If we can't see through the smoke, we can fail. My parents, neighbors, coaches, and mentors are the very reason I had a chance. I missed out on opportunities when I was closed-minded and didn't take my blinders off. With their help, I made decisions with the Mindset of staying on the right side of good.

I turned negative situations into opportunities. I could have easily quit or chosen a different life path. You know the phrase, "When the going gets tough, the tough get going"? Well, this is genuinely the Mindset I had to develop. Even more critical is to ensure that you do things with the honesty of purpose. I have learned how to embrace life and choose the right path and use my experiences to make me better. I know how to look at the surrounding factors and pull from them to create a better me. I've cringed in the dark, cried in the rain, laughed when I wanted, and when it was time to be proud, I knew how to do that, too. I hope that at the end of this book you'll understand how to be a better you.

I will eagerly try to pull out your strengths, relationship-building skills, team-building skills, and, most importantly, understand other people's strengths and where to find opportunities for success. Once you have those understandings, you can formulate these characteristics of Mindset to shape them into Chemistry, Culture, and Heart, which form your Vision and values. I'll use my experiences coaching world-class athletes, my family experiences, and how I brought teams together to win national championships. My goal is to help you find the inner leadership in every team member, so they work great with each person's strengths for the good of all, creating a mindset of winners win when everyone works together. It's the secret sauce to building great, winning teams.

CHEMISTRY: CREATING THE MINDSET

I focus so strongly on chemistry because I know that a solid mutual attachment, an interaction between people working together towards the same goal, is what makes the chemical bond. For example, in building a team, it's crucial to get the right factors together because anyone can have a team, but having the element of chemistry is the most critical key to a winning team. I understood this early in the coaching and recruiting game.

In Michigan, AAU basketball teams were popping up all over the place. Teams were growing because there were not enough positions available on the elite teams. So new team after a new team came and went. Some coaches did not align with winning programs because they did not fit the winning Culture, and they weren't successful. In my experience, Coaches created teams because someone else figured out how to form a better team. After all, players with the wrong Mindset didn't have a home. So teams were created by mom/dad or aunt/uncle.

When selecting team members, it's imperative to correct the team's mission and the team members' mission. As a Coach, it never bothered me to coach against a newly-formed team. Either they'd be better than my team, and we could learn from them, or we'd destroy them. We often beat them. With many AAU teams, the coach's name is the first part of the team's name, which tells me the organization is more about the coach than the team and its Culture.

Regardless of why so many AAU teams were formed, there were way too many teams. The mission of all teams was the same: to have a winning summer program so college coaches could recruit, and the players would have a chance to play the best competition and earn a full-ride scholarship. The players were the commodity.

With so many great players, the key is the right Mindset and who can work as a team. Mindset is the key. Like on any team, we need the right players in the right places, and the faster we understand the mission, the better the results of that team.

In 2010, I was coaching the Michigan Mustangs, an Adidas-sponsored AAU travel basketball team. The program was at a standstill. The Mustangs had been a household name for many years, but we were running on old success. We needed to get with the times and look at our program's chemistry, Culture, and Heart to start forming the Vision and values of a championship team.

My eyes were on the best players with the best basketball IQ, Heart, and team mindset. I started out recruiting players from bad teams. I picked up players off teams we'd beaten. As long as they had the intangibles, I'd recruit them. But most of all, I'd look at how players took losing.

I recruited around Michigan, looking at rankings, ranking sites, going to high school games, driving all over the state--to Detroit, to Grand Rapids, to Flint, to Inkster—to find players who would help build a team with specific winning skills.

The first player I recruited to the national championship team was Josh Kozinski, Edwardsburg High School's all-time leading three-point shooter. Josh had been shooting the lights out from that range since 8th grade. Our Michigan Mustangs played against Josh in Indianapolis while he was on the top-ranked team in the country, the Spiece Indy Heat.

Jeff Kozinski, Josh's dad, was Spiece Indy Heat's assistant coach. I reached out to Jeff and found out our teams played in the same tournament the following weekend. I told him we needed to connect at that venue to discuss Josh and his future. I said I knew how to help Josh reach his maximum potential. I'd analyze his skill set and help him play using his best skills related to the college game. That, in turn, would help Josh get recruited for what he did best. He'd have the freedom to be himself, and I'd build a team to do what he could not, with players that would compliment and highlight his strengths. Not knowing Jeff was also Josh's high school coach, I told him I'd be the best coach his son ever had.

At the tournament, we played against Spiece Indy Heat. They had two of the country's best point guards and one of the best big men ever seen. Unfortunately, they beat us by almost 40 points. Josh didn't play much, and I believed his coach didn't know how to use him. So I told Jeff, "After this season, why not come and play with us. Josh would be the starting shooting guard, and you can be the team's assistant coach." Jeff agreed. Now we just had to convince his wife, Amy, that this was the most beneficial thing for Josh. We had to make sure she knew this was not just two basketball-jock coaches making a decision but that Josh would benefit most.

At the end of that summer, Josh played for us in a tournament and stood out. He had eight three-pointers in the first four minutes of his first Michigan Mustangs game and finished with seventeen total. His shot was outstanding, and he played with Heart. He was not only our starting shooting guard but was our best player.

Josh brought several vital attributes that we needed, including a great basketball IQ and the ability to shoot with extreme range and accuracy. Building a winning team is critically important to know everyone's role, and Josh's was to put points on the board.

In his first game, we played one of those pop-up teams called Southfield Transition. We beat them, but barely. Their star player, Johnathon Williams, had the key attributes of solid shooting ability, the confidence of a leader, and exceptional defensive skills. He was a great player who also had Chemistry, Culture, and Heart. Johnathon went to Southfield Lathrup, my old high school.

To build an elite team, we needed more than one leader. Having Josh was good for us, but I also knew one leader was not enough to win on the big stage. Josh's key attribute of shooting ability would not alone win us games. He needed someone who was able to get him the ball.

Johnathon was that guy. He could handle, shoot, and create for others. And even more importantly, he wanted to play with us. So, he joined the team, and we then had two of Michigan's top scorers. One was the best shooter the state has ever seen, and the other was the best combo guard who could score and handle the pressure of elite play. But what I loved most about Johnathon was his defense.

Even though he could score the ball with the best players in the country, Johnathon was a defensive specialist. He cared about playing defense just as much as he did about putting points on the board. Josh was a shooter, and Johnathon was a scorer who played defense. We were now on our way to having an elite team, and the winning team mindset was rounding out.

4

CULTURE: AAU TRAVEL EXPERIENCE

The team's Chemistry was forming well, but we were still missing the ability to achieve our mission of winning collectively. We needed to build on our Culture.

There was an elite player in the circuit to "see" the floor with his eyes closed--the critical attribute of Vision. So to elevate the team's Culture, my number one target that summer was Derrick Walton, Jr., But I had to have an attractive enough team for him to want to play with us.

We needed role players.

The best role players are the ones who understand their role, do it well, and are willing to sacrifice their wants to give everything for the team's sake. Culture grows from an open mindset and is the ability to see the big picture. A cultural perspective grows when everyone understands how to achieve a common goal as a team.

Derrick was Chandler Park Academy's pass-first point guard who also loved to play defense. I had never coached or even seen a player with his incredible passing and scoring abilities. As a result, I did not get him to play the first, second, or third time I tried.

But I knew that top Michigan high school players attended Michigan or Michigan State football games on fall weekends. I had great relationships with each coaching staff, so I went to U of M hoping to run into Derrick. Instead, I ran into Steve Haney, Jr.

Steve happened to be my next target, so when he said he wanted to play for the Michigan Mustangs and specifically for me, that was the best news I could have heard. He was a 6'8" shooting guard with excellent ball-handling skills, so of course, I gladly welcomed him to our team. I have to admit that I didn't go to the game thinking I would solidify his addition to the Mustangs that day.

With the addition of Steve Haney, we now had two shooting guards who were top-ranked in the country. I asked Steve who he thought was the best point guard in Michigan to run our team at the football game. He said, "Derrick Walton." I agreed then asked how we could get him to play for us. He said, "Oh, we'll get him. That's one of my best friends." He gave me Derrick Senior's phone number, so I called Derrick Junior's father later that day. Derrick Senior wanted to meet me in person before talking with his son. So two days later, I drove from Kalamazoo down to Chandler Park to watch Derrick at practice and talk to his dad on the east side of Detroit. They were both committed to the Mustangs after that meeting.

Good recruiters know they need to get both parents involved and committed whenever possible. They need to help them have an open mind to what's possible if their child takes an opportunity to be a part of a team. Additionally, if the mother is locked in, the player will be committed. Before getting Derrick to play with the Michigan Mustangs, I spoke to Angela, Derrick's mother. She was the final decision, and her husband and I wanted to make sure she was comfortable with having Derrick on the team.

Derrick Walton joined the Michigan Mustangs in the summer of 2010. We could now compete at the highest level. We beat some outstanding teams; we even beat teams we should not have been able to compete with. It had started. Our team was attractive. We were building a winning formula: Vision and core values around Culture, Chemistry, and Heart.

5

RECRUITING VS.
BEING SELECTED

After the 2010 season, we went back to the drawing board. We'd built a competitive team, but we weren't consistently winning, and we wanted to win the whole summer. My assistant coaches, Jeff Kozinski and Van Mayfield, were pleased with the 2010 season, but we knew we had to get a few more players. They had their eyes on another high-level player, Deandre Johnson. Dre's key attributes were shooting ability, ball-handling, and court vision. He was a Top 10 point guard in Michigan.

After this pickup, I started to feel like we could not only compete but win. In addition to our usual schedule, we played tournaments in Texas, Michigan, and Indiana, followed by a tournament in Las Vegas to end the summer. We won several local tournaments, but at the more significant events, we struggled badly.

At the end of the summer, I told the team we'd had a great season, but we had to get better. We needed to add size. Steve was the tallest player on the team, but he was a shooting guard. We had no inside presence. There were many big men committed to other teams, and since the Mustangs had the best guards in the Midwest, I couldn't just select anyone. We needed a big man who had our Mindset of Chemistry, Culture, and Heart. We had good role players, but they hadn't fully developed the Vision of a winning team. They didn't understand their role if they were not the number one option to score because they were used to being the scorer.

I knew their Mindset would not align with Culture, Chemistry, and Heart if we couldn't create the Vision they needed. Building a team's core values is the hardest part of forming a championship team. It is imperative to select role players. The best role players are the ones who understand their role, do it well, and are willing to sacrifice their wants and give everything for the team's sake.

At the end of that summer, I was at home in Kalamazoo when I got a knock at the door, followed by a doorbell ring. It was a kid selling cookies for his AAU basketball team. He was 6'9", built like a Ford Truck, very well-spoken, and humble. I asked him what team he played for, and he said Bank Hoops. I told him I coached the Michigan Mustangs and would love to have him on my team. He said, "Yeah, we beat y'all two years ago." I told him that would never happen again and that if he joined the Mustangs, I'd help him get a basketball scholarship. He dropped the cookies and told his dad he wanted to play for me. And that's how Malichi Satterlee became a Mustang. What set him apart from others was humility. He didn't mind doing all the little stuff, like going door to door selling cookies. Willingness to do the little stuff is a critical trait of a role player. He was a great addition to Derrick, Steve, Josh, and Dre. They all loved him because he had so many key attributes they didn't. It created the chemistry the team needed because they had to rely on each other.

We still needed more inside presence. With Mali, we could compete but not win. My favorite big guy in the circuit was Jalen Hayes, who played for a pop-up team named Dorian's Pride, a 16U team in our same age division. He had the missing key attributes we needed for a winning team. A big guy who played like a guard, was faster and more mobile than other bigs. During the high school season, he played for Lansing Sexton in Lansing, Michigan, the crosstown rival of Lansing Eastern, Steve Haney, Jr's school.

When Eastern played Sexton, I got the other Mustangs to come out in support. Then, at the end of the game, we all went up to Jalen and told him he'd make the difference on our team. At 6'8", he could pass, create shots on the inside, and rebound outside his area. He was the Derrick Walton of the post. We had a great post presence but needed to have a player to back up Mali and Jalen.

The coaches knew we could either make it happen in the summer of 2011 or wait until 2012 to select the final big player. We chose to wait to get the right player. We knew we could do a lot with the guys we had and didn't want to overdo it. So, with hopes of winning the big championship of the summer, we played 2011 with the players we had. In Las Vegas, we made the Final Eight but didn't have enough to finish on top. We ran into a team called New York New Heights. They had guards who were just as tough as ours and four guys like Mali who were more robust than Jalen. We lost, but we had room to build. New York went on to win the 2011 National Championship. This only affirmed what I already knew I needed.

6

THE WINNING TEAM:

The 2012 high school season was the most critical part of my AAU coaching career. Playing the Adidas travel circuit had taught me everything I needed to know. I especially knew I needed to get role players inside who were more prominent than Mali and stronger than Jalen. So I had the game plan and drove to Saginaw, Flint, and Detroit, looking for the most demanding players the state had to offer who would fit that plan.

A good friend of mine who coached at Lansing Eastern held a Thanksgiving Day scrimmage featuring all of Michigan's best high school players. There, I knew I'd find the players I needed.

Derrick, Steve, and Jalen wanted me to recruit Monte "Man Man" Morris. He and Derrick were ranked the number one and number two point guards on everybody's list, but who was first and second were highly debated. So although Man Man had all the qualities we wanted, the coaches and I didn't decide on him. But we did watch him all afternoon.

Another player everyone wanted to add to the team was Fredrick Edmonds. Everyone knew him as "Boo Man" because he was the bully that bullied the bullies, the ghost who scared everyone. Unfortunately, I didn't find what I knew I needed to win the championship in these two players. At that point, I hadn't seen anything I was looking for.

We held tryouts for the Michigan Mustangs' 2012 season in the spring. There was a lot of buzz about us possibly having D Walt and

Man Man on the team. While recruiting them, I never chose who was best because they were completely different players and considerable talents. Everywhere I went, I was questioned about how I would handle who would run the point. I told people that was not my focus. My focus was on molding the team's Culture. At the time, people looked at me as if I was the craziest person in the world, but that changed months later.

Our coaching staff knew we wanted to build a team with the winning Mindset of Culture, Chemistry, and Heart. So when recruiting, we spent time focused on building these areas one player at a time. Once we figured out who had the pillars of the championship mindset, we designed our team. That meant every player we put on the court would need to represent our vision and core values to be a winner.

We got a commitment from Man Man during his school basketball season. I talked with his mom about the opportunities ahead of him, and she put a stamp on the deal. A lanky, skinny kid with a quirky-looking jump shot, he had the Heart of a lion. He had an old-school game but was a passing and scoring point guard.

So now my dilemma was making sure Derrick and Man Man heard *my* voice, not the entire State of Michigan's. I pulled them into the office during the first practice and told them they'd never have to worry about competing playing time at the point. I made sure they knew the only thing that mattered on this team was them both leading us to wins.

At the time, Norm Oden, president, and CEO of the Michigan Mustangs, told me in his wise, older-man voice, "Damon, here are my thoughts …You will destroy this team. Too many people are pitting these two-point guards against each other. It's such a short season, and you won't be able to get their buy-in. There's no way you can win with two-point guards, three small guards, two undersized shooting guards, and undersized big men."

April of 2012 was the start of the Best Summer Ever. A week before the first tournament, Derrick Senior called me to say Derrick would be attending the USA High School Basketball Camp. I was very proud and happy for him. We traveled to our first event, in Detroit, with everyone but Derrick. We went through the tournament beating all our opponents by 40 points or more. We then ran into the Nike Family, a team that had killed us every time we played them.

Every Nike Family player was at the top of every ranking. Unfortunately, our team still had doubts, and they looked to me to tell me what they were capable of doing. But we had Culture, Chemistry, and Heart, and we had players with Vision and core values. Everyone's key attributes combined on the floor, allowing us to play like I never thought we could. The team, now comprised of Man Man, Josh, Dre, Steve, Johnathon, Boo Man, and Jalen Hayes, gave us what they had, and we were winning late in the game. Monte Morris stood out like no other—shooting, scoring, passing, and doing it all. Jonathan Williams did everything I knew he could. Josh Kozinski and Steve Haney shot the ball better than any other players I'd ever coached, and yet we ended up losing by four points. I will never forget that feeling. I wanted to play the game again because I felt like I'd lost it by not having the "Heart" I had built our team around.

After that first tournament, people questioned us because we'd lost to Nike, the powerhouse in Michigan for many years. We were supposed to be the new powerhouse. For me, that game created a new rivalry, partly because A high school friend of mine coached with Nike. "Smoke" and I had grown up playing ball together, and now here we were. He was the powerhouse, and I was the underdog. It was our time to beat him, and I was supposed to have one of the best teams in the country, and I lost.

At that moment, I brought the team into a huddle and told them not to worry about that loss. To be great, we would have to lose. The most important thing was to learn from our failures. I told those guys that any team that beat us would never beat us twice. It was up to us to know how we'd lost the first time, so we'd never be outplayed or outcoached the second time. No one would ever outperform us in a rematch. But sometimes, we had to go through things to make sure we understand how to attack the game.

We had an opportunity to face the Nike family again at one of the country's most prestigious tournaments, Spiece, in Fort Wayne, Indiana. Of course, all of the great teams played at Spiece, and any that wanted to be considered a top team would have to dominate there. But, of course, the same went for individual players who wanted to be considered the best.

The tournament features the most games played on a single day in AAU basketball, six. So by the end of the day, my guys were exhausted. But we'd made it to the championship game, and the team on the other side of the bracket was Nike Family.

In AAU basketball, only championship games are played on Sunday, so getting to that day is a fantastic feat. However, after Game 5 of Day 1, Derrick, Jalen, and Jon Jon were cramping up from their necks to their toes. Fortunately, Boo Man and Man Man were ready to play. Boo Man said to me, "Don't worry about it. I got it this time, Coach. I'll make sure that we win."

Of course, in my head, I'm thinking, "How are we going to beat these guys when we already gave everything we had?" Also, everybody had performed at peak ability the first time we'd played Nike, and we'd lost. Now, it was time for us to face them again, and we were beaten.

I checked myself and my emotions at the door. We didn't have Derrick, but I wasn't going to let that be why the team didn't rise to the occasion. I knew we had Heart.

As it turned out, Nike's coach wanted to forfeit the final because his players were tired and had cramps. He said they could not compete. We were ready to play with what we had, so we took the championship home with us on the forfeit.

Sometimes wins come in unconventional ways. We'd wanted to compete, and they could not. That was not our fault. So, we were Spiece champions. We'd won the biggest event of the summer because we'd had the Heart to play despite our physical challenges. This experience taught us that everybody needed to be ready, even when a teammate was down.

Before we headed home, we huddled in the parking lot, and I told the team again that we wouldn't lose to any team twice. I was sorry that Nike's players couldn't, for whatever reason, play the final game. But a win was a win, and we were taking it.

People started to recognize the chemistry between Derrick Walton and Monte Morris. As two of the country's most elite players, they built our team culture through their co-leadership. Reporters started to ask how I could pull these two players together and have success with two-point guards, how their demand for the ball wasn't destroying the team. I continued to tell the press and people that followed us that it was our Culture, chemistry, and Heart. I consistently poured into Derrick and Man Man that we would win as long as they believed in our three pillars.

This team bought into the Mindset from Day One. We went around the country beating elite teams. We beat a host of players we had no business competing with. The New York teams had the best point guards. The Florida teams with the tallest, strongest, biggest athletes in the country. We beat the country farm boys from Iowa. We beat them all because we had great Culture, Chemistry, and Heart. Our two-point guards set the tone, and we went on to win the national championship—the Adidas Super 64—in Las Vegas at the end of the summer. It was the first time in modern history that a Michigan team went out of state and brought back a national championship.

We had a great time getting there, and the ultimate reward for a phenomenal season was winning it all in a game played on ESPN. Every player on the roster got a basketball scholarship. They all did their role and held to our words. They showed up on the big stage and showed what can happen if you remove ego and titles and focus on a mission and Mindset around Chemistry, Culture, and Heart. They led the nation to accomplish anything when you keep true to the team's vision and core values.

The Michigan Mustangs were victorious because we identified skill sets. We identified roles and did the best we could in those roles. And we knew we would lose games, but nobody would ever beat us twice. That held everybody accountable--me as a coach, my assistant coaches, the club's president, and everyone involved with our team. We held each other accountable so that we could grow together and be great as a unit.

7

TESTING THE CHAMPIONSHIP THEORY

The Michigan Mustangs coaching structure was organized to start at the 15U level and then stay with their team until they were 17U. Then each coach would start back at 15U. This seemed logical, but parents and players all wanted to work with the person who got it done, which they assumed was me. I was just one who bought into the formula of Culture, Chemistry, and Heart. I knew that anyone could win using it. The problem was recruiting all of the players. I did my part by recruiting for the entire program. Then, when it was time to take visits, I did. I spoke to parents, but each coach had his unique talent, as well. I just did what I knew how to do best.

The program did ok the first year after we won the national championship. Each coach focused on Culture, Chemistry, and Heart, but the second year after the title, our program was not at the championship level, so Adidas considered us struggling. Then, we started getting calls from Adidas saying they'd take our sponsorship if we didn't win or have players the college coaches wanted.

I knew we had to do something, and I talked to the coaches and our president. I looked at everyone's teams to ensure we had the Derrick Waltons and Monte Morrises, the Boo Mans and Joshs of the world on each team. We had to have leaders and a great core of role players that would sacrifice for the group's good. We had a team meeting and set out a game plan for getting the players we needed. We had our number one targets on each roster. It was time for me to get to work.

I helped recruit Austin Davis, who's currently playing for the University of Michigan. I put in a considerable effort to get Brian "Tug" Bowen, who now plays for the Indiana Pacers. Those were our headliners for the 17U team. Then we had to get the best role players we could. I was coaching the 16U team, and we had everything that we needed and wanted. For the 15U team, I recruited a coach who had a team but no funding. So, we brought on a coach named James Valler. His son was a pretty good point guard, and he had a kid named Duane Washington, Jr. A smaller, chunky guard, Duane could shoot the lights out and had a great work ethic. So, they also had the keys to making a good team--two outstanding players and a whole group of supporting cast members that would fit the program's Mindset.

8

YOU MUST SHARE YOUR LEADERSHIP

I had to rebuild for a different reason and in another way, but using the same model. My 16U team was Number 1 in the country, and we won many championships. We had our headliners and our role players and were again the talk of the circuit. Both our 17U and 15U teams were ranked in the Top 5 nationally. We had Jermaine Jackson, Jr., and Foster Loyer for point guards. Matthew Beachler, Dylan Alderson, and Demetrius Lake were all scoring guards with individual key attributes. We had size with James Beck, Jack Ballingtine, Xavier Tillman (Grizzles), and Isiah Livers (Michigan Mr. Basketball) all on the inside. We had it all. We did it again—we traveled the nation and won.

The following summer, my son, Damon, Jr., said he wanted me to coach him. At the time, a college friend was coaching DJ's team. I went to watch DJ play, and he wasn't getting off the bench. I had a talk with the coach after the game, and he looked me in the eye and said, "He's just not that good."

When he put DJ in a game, I saw what he was talking about. It was like nothing I'd ever seen. DJ couldn't make layups and didn't know how to play defense. I understood why he wasn't playing.

That next year, I shocked the AAU world and stopped coaching the older group. Yes, the number one team in the country, with players who were the cream of the crop. I had to give my son the same commitment I was giving other players. Everybody was looking forward to us winning the National Championship, but at the time, my son was more important to me than anything else. I'd hated watching that game when he wasn't good, knowing I could help him. I'd told him after I'd seen him play that, the following year, he and I would start going to the YMCA to work on his basketball skills. So, I stepped down from coaching the elite team to keep my word.

One evening after work, I went to pick DJ up from school to go to the gym. He was not good at the time, and we had a hurdle to jump through. But, like everyone else, I wanted my son to be one of the best players on the team. So I turned to him and said, "I don't know what we're going to do at this point. What are your thoughts?"

DJ suggested we start working out at 5 A.M. when nobody would be at the gym. I thought that was a good idea, except that he had to be at school by 7:00, and I had to be at work by 8:00. So to get to the gym when it opened at 5:00 A.M., we'd have to get up by 4:00.

DJ said, "I'll go to bed early."

Four years later, DJ and I were consistent. At 5:00 A.M., we worked on ball handling, layups, jump shots, defense--on every aspect of the game.

His seventh-grade year was the first opportunity to make a basketball team--at Linden Grove Middle School. The coach was a man I'd coached against when I had powerhouse teams, and we'd beaten them badly every time we played. So, I was nervous that I had a kid who wasn't that good and a coach who probably didn't like me determining my kid's destiny.

He did choose my son to be on the team, and. So DJ and I continued to go to the gym at 5 A.M. I was one of those obsessed dads. I went to the game, and I analyzed the plays; I took DJ to the gym the following day. I taught him how to score in plays and how to be a player who'd stand out on a team.

DJ was now considered one of the best players not only in his class but in Kalamazoo. By eighth grade, he was one of the starting shooting guards.

This rebuild showed me DJ was missing something from the formula—Vision. I saw a person who didn't believe in himself but believed in me. My son admired the work I was doing with other players but didn't think he had it in him to be one. So we continued to work, and DJ ended up being one of those players, a player coaches wanted on their team. He was also recognized as one of the Top 25 freshmen in Michigan when he entered high school. He played in elite tournaments and was invited to camps where he talked to influential coaches. I was proud of my son. He was doing it.

Now, DJ's playing varsity basketball at Oswego East High School in Illinois and looking to receive college scholarship offers. Knowing where he started, we're pleased to know some colleges are considering him.

Sometimes in life, we do what's easy. But sometimes, our current situation is setting us up to be able to handle more significant challenges. In this scenario, I had to make some sacrifices. I'm thankful I did, and not only for DJ's sake. I realized my commitment to helping him was incredibly important to him. He was no longer on the sidelines watching others play. He needed to be coached and developed like the other players I'd coached in the Michigan Mustangs.

We owe our teams, friends, and co-workers our best and our special talents. When we have identified our strengths and leadership traits, it's important to share them. The reason we owe that to others is that others have given their time and talents to us. We are who we are because someone shared their leadership with us. Now, it's our turn to share. It is our responsibility to make sure that we coach, guide, develop, and lead someone.

DJ and I came up with a goal together; we processed it together; we executed it together. I sacrificed for my son, as we all should sacrifice for our families, jobs, and the people around us.

Your skills and qualities may get you there, but your Mindset and focus on your vision and core values create the right formula for winning. Sharing your leadership is the ultimate way to make sure you're not at the top alone.

9

FULL CIRCLE

I was a teacher, teaching Microsoft Office and wanting to be in leadership, and I knew what to look for in a team: Culture, Chemistry, somewhere to commit myself to, and a place where they would let me show my Heart. I found Southwest Michigan First (SWMF), an organization whose primary mission is to create jobs, attract employers, develop talent and drive economic development and investment in the region. SWMF was a fantastic place to work because it had all of the working formulas. Had I been closed-minded and didn't understand the things that made me happy in the work environment, then I would have never met my life's mentor or learned about the importance of continuous growth.

I was able to have experienced at work where I could impact and influence people's lives and help them reach their dreams. I worked hard to become a community leader by using the same formulas with community members with my championship basketball teams.

If you know what the end game is, you'll be able to apply the winning skill traits, like in my examples of selecting a winning culture, then finding people with the right heartbeats, and applying Heart and commitment. I found that when you are winning the right way, it's fun. It's going to have its share of challenges, but it will be fun. I call not enjoying your time coaching, working, or just living "doing time." It's like doing things against your will because you decided to approach life the wrong way. If asked to "do time," would you volunteer? Of course not. It's up to you to share your leadership and attack life with the formula.

10

HAVE BALANCE OR "DO TIME." YOUR CHOICE:

Burnout is real! If we're looking to keep helping ourselves and the people around us, we need to understand the piece of the formula called balance. Creating a balance gives you a sense of peace and time to get life's stresses off your mind. For example, basketball gives me the amount of exercise I need, brotherhood, and time with friends. It's also competitive and result-driven.

In my first few years of marriage, I'd come home from work and be kind of uptight from things that had happened there or just daily stresses. When Chelsea saw me like that, my wife would say, "There has to be open basketball run somewhere at somebody's gym." She made sure I took notice that I was bringing lousy energy home. She had it figured out. If I were in a bad place, she'd offer up basketball and more time with the fellas to get me the balance I needed. Years later, I still apply the same thoughts to action. Whenever I'm frustrated, I ask myself how much time am I spending around basketball, or have I been to the movies with my family, or have we taken a short vacation. Or am I just "doing time"?

When I worked at SWMF, our CEO always asked about our personal lives. At first, I thought it was a little weird, but what he was doing was making sure I was doing more than just work. I currently work at Zeigler Automotive Group as a Corporate Recruiter and Talent

Development Leader. We have a thing called Friday Positives. During this weekly recap, we talk about things we're doing with our families or just personally that show we're not just doing time.

Both of these companies are champions of Culture. Both value work-life balance. Both thrive and make the "Best and Brightest Companies to Work For" list year after year. These two powerhouse organizations know what matters—people! They get it! They both invest in others' success. The **Culture** is there, the **Chemistry** of being one is there, **committed** to the education of their current staff and their leaders, and their employees have **Heart**. When you have these traits, you'll find that work doesn't have to feel like you're doing time. It becomes working with a family in the workplace. I'm living proof that when you leave a company that cares about not just "doing time," you miss it deeply.

My wife accepted a promotion, and our family relocated to Illinois. I had to find a job. I was looking online, calling hiring firms, asking companies what they believed about home and work-life balance, about their Culture, about their chemistry, and their team's Heart. As you can probably imagine, I didn't have much success.

However, the owner of Zeigler Automotive Group was on the board of Southwest Michigan First. I noticed he had a franchise in Illinois, and that's how I joined Zeigler's fantastic team.

Since being with the company, I've developed a curriculum for leadership growth and development. I was allowed to write a program and implement it with over 1800 company employees. That's important because it meant I was bringing my talents to the Zeigler team. I love that I get to continue to live in a world where people care about what you do in your personal life, just as they care about your work life.

11

TRANSITION:

During the lockdown, it happened: I got a call informing me there wasn't any work available, and there was a layoff. I had to figure out what to do moving forward. Being furloughed from Zeigler was the most frightening thing at the time. We had to depend on a broken and crowded unemployment system. Since being happy had always been important to us, that would now be my focus. I had to find out what made us happy, energized, and inspired during the layoff and lockdown.

Trying to figure out what makes us happy started with thinking out loud to my wife and kids. An excellent question was asked: When I am at my most empowered self, which things are consistent? Our family's answer was working out, reading, and being close to the Church.

DJ and I went right away to the basement. We converted our huge basement storage room into a weight room. We mounted a TV and brought the big boom-box in so we'd have loud music. I went out and bought a treadmill, weight bench, elliptical, yoga mats, and yoga balls, and we were all set for working out. Other things that made the kids happy were, of course, phones and video games. My oldest wanted to have her phone twenty-four hours a day. My middle son just wanted to sleep, eat, play games, and sleep again. My twins wanted video games every day. My responsibility was to help them stay focused and forward-thinking.

Along with the rest of the country, my family was on edge. And we had questions. Was school going to be canceled for the whole year? Were all sports and, most importantly, basketball going to be canceled for DJ? Should we allow, the twins to go back to school when appropriate, since they'd otherwise miss out on everything that meant being elementary students: plays, games, gym class, interactions with classmates.

This was a challenging time for us. I had to arrange and schedule our day where we could all "checkboxes" to feel like our lives hadn't stopped. We needed to stay encouraged. So, I rolled out a plan on Sunday night after dinner. I told the older two kids I'd be waking them up at 7 A.M. so we could start unpacking the day. Then we'd wake up the twins and give them their day's schedule.

Next, we'd clean the kitchen and their rooms, then make sure nothing had carried over from the previous day. Once they were working, it was time for me to pour into myself. When the kids were off doing chores, I'd be listening to a podcast or paying bills.

We'd have lunch, clean one more time, then watch a movie. The kids would let me choose the movies until I kept picking old gangster films. After movie time, I'd cook dinner. Everyone had to work out in some form and fashion seven days a week, but weekends were their time. They could hang out and be lazy teenagers if they wanted.

We were ready for the Covid 19 lockdown. We had the Allison Family Plan. We were going to stay in shape, become closer, and be more innovative than we were before the lockdown started.

We were doing a great job at the plan, and it worked for our family. The kids were getting their work done, and I was turning into a great chef. I prepared three meals a day, and everyone was meeting and achieving their workout and educational goals. In addition, everyone was getting time to themselves to do their "thing" on the weekends.

My wife, on the other hand, as an essential worker, had to be at work at 7:00 A.M. and work until 6:30 P.M. or later. I'd get up every morning and help her out the door, just with a kiss or coffee. She was trying to save the world, keep people employed, keep her job, and stay positive at work. She was responsible for many people's livelihoods.

Week three of the lockdown, my daughter got a track scholarship to Indiana Tech. Not only was that awesome for her, but it was also impactful for all of us. It kept us aware that life will continue after this time. Finally, we had something to celebrate, which was monumental for our family. My first child had a college scholarship.

12

THOUGHTS ABOUT BALANCE:

I have also worked for a company that didn't focus on me as a person. They didn't care if their workers were doing time. I was frustrated working day after day in this toxic situation. If employees took a vacation, it was frowned upon. Everyone just did their job, just wanted to make the deadline and present their part. There was no team chemistry. I did time for over thirteen years in that job. My employers did not give the impression that they knew or cared about the winning "formula." I missed my daughter's 5th-grade graduation. I missed my son's youth games. I missed a whole era of my family's life because this organization didn't understand how to win.

Now, when I talk to colleagues from that job, they wonder why I'm always so happy. They wonder how I have time to go to my kid's games and how I get to do so many amazing things at work. I explain that I'm focused on "not doing time" on finding my balance, which may be lifting weights, playing basketball, or just being around people who share the "winning formula."

I try to explain to friends from my previous career that doing things that make them happy is the only way to reach their maximum potential. We are creatures of habit. So, we have to be thoughtful in doing things that create an outstanding balance.

My father-in-law, Jerry Fry, says that we don't have to be who we were raised to be. We can pivot, adapt, and overcome. I was raised traditionally. We had just the basics. You know, the wooden spoons, not the silver spoons. Jerry told me I could always change my habits and focus on things that made me and our family happy. That differed from my upbringing. We didn't focus on those things. That wasn't my family's end game. Our end game was survival, and we did it the best way that we could.

Every time Jerry was around us or the kids stayed the night at their grandparent's house, I noticed him giving compliments or just showing love. It all came back around to the same theme: Culture, Chemistry, Commitment, and Heart. I saw the love my kids had for their grandfather. He'd always make them feel special about the little things they were doing. When we'd have dinner, he'd always tell whoever cooked how good the food was. I witnessed what a loving, caring being and a locked-in-on-others person can do for another's success.

Jerry, like me, was a wooden spoon guy. His stories from his upbringing were dreadful. When he told of growing up jumping from family member to family member, we wondered how he became such a positive role model.

The thing with Jerry is that he had an open mind. If he had a closed mind, he would have continued to do something that may not have worked for him. So I believe we have to know what does not work and have the Heart to do the things that matter.

As leaders in this world, there are many one-hit wonders because they are so closed-minded. They may have an idea, but if vision isn't allowed to happen, the idea will never come to be. Jerry is a living example of what it means to be the change. He was raised in a world that should have resulted in him "Doing Time" because he was not raised with the formula, but if he can overcome that upbringing, I know I and others can, too.

13

MINDSET

When I interviewed for a position at SWMF, the CEO did not interview me. The people at SWMF did. I met first with a team of seven, then a team of four, then the CEO certified me and welcomed me onto the winning team. Because I did not know what they were looking for, the interview process was tough. Later, I learned that they were looking for someone with a mindset that included Chemistry, Culture, and Heart. It was their "winning formula."

My job at SWMF was to get small business owners to join the Chamber. I was responsible for hosting networking events that included food and beer. I also hosted breakfasts where business owners could connect and discuss growing their footprint in the community. My job was to bring folks together to converse and grow.

This was one of the best opportunities I've ever had. SWMF CEO Ron Kitchens is and will forever be one of my mentors and leadership figures. He showed me how to be a leader better than any leadership class I've taken. He allowed me to see what the formula looked like in a work environment. This organization did it right. They had the right Mindset of the winning Culture.

I learned so much at SWMF that shaped my life and changed my Heart. The organization focused on creating jobs for people so they could change the trajectory of their lives. Ron's motto was "The Greatest Force for Change is a Job." By going to after-hours networking events, I was helping people fulfill their passion. They started small businesses and wanted to connect with other like-minded community members to grow their business. I had a position to bring people together, inspire, impact and influence change in a fun way.

We had a very inspirational book club. I'd sometimes take the book we were reading home to my family, and we'd read it. At an annual event called Catalyst University, I met world leaders who were making a difference. Ron visualized this event, an opportunity to invite inspirational speakers from all over the world to address our community better. Thousands attended, and speakers included John Collins (*Good to Great*) and Bob Beaudine (*The Power of Who*). I was able to reach as far as I wanted to go. I worked side by side with the mayor of Kalamazoo and was on many different community boards. I was the leader I wanted to be, amazed this was my job and had a great total compensation and benefits package.

If I had been closed-minded, I would never have gotten such an experience. I grew into someone my mom would not even have recognized. By having an open mind and being willing to listen to Ron, I ended my career at SWMF as Vice President of the Chamber of Commerce and Partner in Economic Development. I received six promotions in five years.

14

HAVING PARENTS WITH HEART

I was born in Detroit, the second of five children. I have three brothers and one sister. My mother, Darlene, is a Registered Nurse. My dad, Harold, is now retired.

Back in the day, like most people in Detroit without a college degree, my dad worked in a factory. Mom worked 12-hour shifts as a nurse and as much overtime as she could fit in. They always said that they worked so hard to have a different life than what their parents gave them. Mom believed that each generation should be better than the previous one. Her parents showed them all they knew, and my parents gave us all they knew how to give so that we could be significant.

Harold Allison, Sr.

My dad gave me a gift that helps in leadership—the gift of appearance. He taught me that first impressions are always lasting impressions. Passing the "eye test" is huge when someone is in a leadership role.

As a kid, I watched my dad dress up and get ready for Church, work, or just going over to Granny's house to play cards. He also introduced us to spray starch. He used spray starch to crease his jeans and shirts. When he did his hair, it was done perfectly. Not one strand was out of line. He used to tell us that people are judging you when they look at you, and you may not even know it. He wanted us always to look presentable. So when we had on jogging pants, they were clean, matching top and matching socks. When we came home from school, we put our school clothes away and put our clean play clothes on.

Dad's example has stayed with me because I believe how you present yourself is how society will view you and how you'll perform. Demonstrating professional appearance in the workforce means you take the time to shower, iron your clothes, and groom yourself, so you'll feel like a professional and professionally present yourself.

Body type doesn't matter. Presentation is just making sure you give your appearance a tune-up before you leave your house.

My current morning routine is to select my clothes, make sure there are no wrinkles, choose a matching belt to hold my pants up, tuck my shirt in, and last but not least, spray a dab of cologne on my shirt—not too much but, just enough. The cologne is the lagniappe. My dad taught me how to walk into any room and have confidence in myself by the way I dressed.

Darlene Allison

My mom gave us a different life lesson, in work ethic and sacrifice. She showed us how finding passion in a career would make it easy to do the job. Mom worked as a nurse at Detroit Receiving Hospital for over thirty years. She now works at the VA hospital in Southfield, Michigan, as an essential worker.

In her line of work, especially in a big city, Mom has seen accident victims, gunshot victims, victims of domestic violence, death, and much more. I couldn't understand why she wanted to go to work every day. I'd have been miserable. I asked her why she liked her job so much, and she said she was saving people's lives and people depended on her. There is that Mindset again. She knew her end game.

Before she was a nurse, we lived in one of the worst parts of Detroit. Some streets on the city blocks had more vacant lots than houses. Nearly all of my friends were on food stamps and shared the same struggles in life. My mom said she was fed up with food stamps.

She hated going to the grocery store and having to pull out the "funny-colored money" to get groceries. One day at the grocery store, a lady in front of her had a checkbook. My mom thought it was the funny-colored money for a second, but the lady proceeded to write on it and give it to the cashier. Mom decided she was going to get a checkbook and get off food stamps. She started her journey.

She got her RN degree from Henry Ford Community College, doing whatever it took to complete the program. She took us to classes with her, which showed us sacrifice and let us know that it was up to us to get it if we wanted something. Mom worked tirelessly, spending many late hours up reading, not partying, not hanging out, just keeping her eyes on the "checkbook."

Because of Mom's working as a nurse, we moved to Southfield, the "middle class" capital of Detroit. I attended Southfield-Lathrup High School, a vast melting pot of socioeconomic backgrounds and a constant reminder of what or who you could become. This change created my fight and my drive. I didn't want to be the person holding the funny money, and I knew that being lazy wouldn't help me.

I earned a basketball scholarship to American International College (AIC) and just had to pass the ACT with a score of 20 or higher to sign my national letter of intent. Because of my Dyslexia, test-taking was not easy. I had to put into action what I'd learned from my mom. Her long nights of studying rather than having fun and her locking in to make sure I got my dream of playing college basketball showed me the way. After taking the test four times, I got the score I needed.

My older brother, Harold, Jr., had attended American International, but before I signed my letter of intent, I went on one last campus visit. I didn't get the vibe that this would be my new home, so I talked to my high school coaches. They told me I was crazy not to take the scholarship. I told them my mom loved her job because she was doing the work she wanted to do and saving people's lives. I didn't love Massachusetts, where AIC is located. I didn't want to go there.

My coaches suggested another option—Eastern Kentucky

University, in Richmond, Kentucky. I took the visit because I wanted to figure out if I'd be happy doing my job there. A week before school started, I went down with a local player who had signed with EKU. I tried out, earned a scholarship, and played for the Colonels in 1998-99, but I didn't like it there, either.

It didn't work out for me at EKU, but I was determined to find the right fit. So, I transferred to Oakland Community College, then to Saginaw Valley, then to Wayne State University, then to Kalamazoo Valley Community College. Finally, in Kalamazoo, Western Michigan University, I graduated with my bachelor's degree in Elementary Education and a master's degree in Educational Leadership.

15

WHAT BETTER TIME THAN NOW?

Our country is currently going through the COVID-19 Pandemic and racial injustice, just to name two crises. And we are the most divided I have ever seen in my forty-one years on Earth.

Whites, Blacks, and all races have suffered deaths, been alone and scared, and faced countless hardships during this time. I want the country to be united and working together for a common cause, like my Mustangs basketball teams or like the employees at SWMF or Zeigler.

I've started creating small circles of friends to connect with and begin applying my formula. I'm finding people in these circles who are like the Derrick Waltons, Monte Morrises, Xavier Tillmans, and Isaiah Livers of the world. I'm searching for leaders, the people who lead with their hearts.

I'm also searching for the core group who will be the foot-soldiers, the role players to help get this crazy world in order. I'm looking to surround myself with people who share the same winning values. I want a world where hate is not allowed, science matters, and we can all win together. We have work to do, but we can do it.

Who's up for the challenge?

TEAMS THAT IMPACTED ME:

Kalamazoo Public Schools:
KPS gave me insight into that reading and writing are essential. I have my Master's Degree, and the superintendent told me that apart from being in leadership, you need to understand how to read and write. At the time, I struggled with writing, and they would not give me the opportunity because of my Dyslexia. This lack of opportunity gave me motivation.

Southwest Michigan First:
Ron Kitchens and team showed me what investing in other people does to your Heart. Ron Kitchens showed me how to be a leader. He told me that I have a story to tell and encouraged me to share my story in the leadership space. He never judged me on my Dyslexia or things out of my control.

Zeigler Auto Group:
Aaron Zeigler and Mike Van Ryn gave me so many opportunities and believed in me so much that they allowed me to Develop a Leadership course to inspire 1800 employees. They believed in me enough to know that my Heart bleeds, Culture Chemistry & Heart. I am currently working with Michigan, Indiana, and Chicago, building leaders, because of the trust of Mike and Aaron.

Printed in the United States
by Baker & Taylor Publisher Services